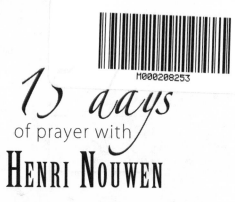

15 days
of prayer with
HENRI NOUWEN

15 days
of prayer/series

On a journey, it's good to have a guide. Even great saints took spiritual directors or confessors with them on their itineraries toward sanctity. Now you can be guided by the most influential spiritual figures of all time. The 15 Days of Prayer series introduces their deepest and most personal thoughts.

This popular series is perfect if you are looking for a gift, or if you want to be introduced to a particular guide and his or her spirituality. Each volume contains:

- cs A brief biography of the saint or spiritual leader
- cs A guide to creating a format for prayer or retreat
- cs Fifteen meditation sessions with focus points and reflection guides

15 days
of prayer with
HENRI NOUWEN

ROBERT WALDRON

NEW CITY PRESS
Hyde Park, NY

Published in the United States by New City Press
202 Cardinal Rd., Hyde Park, NY 12538
www.newcitypress.com
©2009 Robert Waldron

Cover design by Durva Correia

Library of Congress Cataloging-in-Publication Data:

Waldron, Robert G.
  15 days of prayer with Henri Nouwen / by Robert Waldron.
     p. cm.
  Includes bibliographical references (p. 123).
  ISBN 978-1-56548-324-8 (pbk. : alk. paper) 1. Nouwen, Henri J. M.
—Meditations. 2. Spiritual life—Catholic Church.
I. Title. II. Title: Fifteen days of prayer with Henri Nouwen.
  BX4705.N87W33 2009
  242—dc22   2009021056

Printed in the United States of America

Contents

How to Use
This Book

*A*n old Chinese proverb, or at least what I am able to recall of what is supposed to be an old Chinese proverb, goes something like this: "Even a journey of a thousand miles begins with a single step." When you think about it, the truth of the proverb is obvious. It is impossible to begin any project, let alone a journey, without taking the first step. I think it might also be true, although I cannot recall if another Chinese proverb says it, "that the first step is often the hardest." Or, as someone else once observed, "the distance between a thought and the corresponding action needed to implement the idea takes the most energy." I don't know who shared that perception with me but I am certain it was not an old Chinese master!

With this ancient proverbial wisdom, and the not-so-ancient wisdom of an unknown contemporary sage still fresh, we move from

proverbs to presumptions. How do these relate
to the task before us?

I am presuming that if you are reading this
introduction it is because you are contemplating
a journey. My presumption is that you are pre-
paring for a spiritual journey and that you have
taken at least some of the first steps necessary
to prepare for this journey. I also presume, and
please excuse me if I am making too many presumptions, that in your preparation for the spiritual journey you have determined that you need
a guide. From deep within the recesses of your
deepest self, there was something that called you
to consider Henri Nouwen as a potential companion. If my presumptions are correct, may I
congratulate you on this decision? I think you
have made a wise choice, a choice that can be
confirmed by yet another source of wisdom, the
wisdom that comes from practical experience.

Even an informal poll of experienced travel-
ers will reveal a common opinion; it is very difficult to travel alone. Some might observe that it
is even foolish. Still others may be even stronger
in their opinion and go so far as to insist that it
is necessary to have a guide, especially when you
are traveling into uncharted waters and into ter-
ritory that you have not yet experienced. I am of
the personal opinion that a traveling companion
is welcome under all circumstances. The thought
of traveling alone, to some exciting destination

without someone to share the journey with does not capture my imagination or channel my enthusiasm. However, with that being noted, what is simply a matter of preference on the normal journey becomes a matter of necessity when a person embarks on a spiritual journey.

The spiritual journey, which can be the most challenging of all journeys, is experienced best with a guide, a companion, or at the very least, a friend in whom you have placed your trust. This observation is not a preference or an opinion but rather an established spiritual necessity. All of the great saints with whom I am familiar had a spiritual director or a confessor who journeyed with them. Admittedly, at times the saints might well have traveled far beyond the experience of their guide and companion but more often than not they would return to their director and reflect on their experience. Understood in this sense, the director and companion provided a valuable contribution and necessary resource. When I was learning how to pray (a necessity for anyone who desires to be a full-time and public "religious person"), the community of men that I belong to gave me a great gift. Between my second and third year in college, I was given a one-year sabbatical, with all expenses paid and all of my personal needs met. This period of time was called novitiate. I was officially designated as a novice, a beginner in the spiritual journey, and I was assigned a "master," a person who was willing to lead me. In addition to the master, I was provided with every imaginable book and any other resource that I could possibly need. Even with all that I was provided, I did not learn how to pray because of the books and the unlimited resources, rather it was the master, the companion who was the key to the experience.

One day, after about three months of reading, of quiet and solitude, and of practicing all of the methods and descriptions of prayer that were available to me, the master called. "Put away the books, forget the method, and just listen." We went into a room, became quiet, and tried to recall the presence of God, and then, the master simply prayed out loud and permitted me to listen to his prayer. As he prayed, he revealed his hopes, his dreams, his struggles, his successes, and most of all, his relationship with God. I discovered as I listened that his prayer was deeply intimate but most of all it was self-revealing. As I learned about him, I was led through his life experience to the place where God dwells. At that moment I was able to understand a little bit about what I was supposed to do if I really wanted to pray.

The dynamic of what happened when the master called, invited me to listen, and then revealed his innermost self to me as he communicated with God in prayer, was important.

It wasn't so much that the master was trying to reveal to me what needed to be said; he was not inviting me to pray with the same words that he used, but rather that he was trying to bring me to that place within myself where prayer becomes possible. That place, a place of intimacy and of self-awareness, was a necessary stop on the journey and it was a place that I needed to be led to. I could not have easily discovered it on my own.

The purpose of the volume that you hold in your hand is to lead you, over a period of fifteen days or, maybe more realistically, fifteen prayer periods, to a place where prayer is possible. If you already have a regular experience and practice of prayer, perhaps this volume can help lead you to a deeper place, a more intimate relationship with the Lord.

It is important to note that the purpose of this book is not to lead you to a better relationship with Henri Nouwen, your spiritual companion. Although your companion will invite you to share some of his deepest and most intimate thoughts, your companion is doing so only to bring you to that place where God dwells. After all, the true measurement of all companions for the journey is that they bring you to the place where you need to be, and then they step back, out of the picture. A guide who brings you to the desired destination and then sticks around is a very unwelcome guest!

Many times I have found myself attracted to a particular idea or method for accomplishing a task, only to discover that what seemed to be inviting and helpful possessed too many details. All of my energy went to the mastery of the details and I soon lost my enthusiasm. In each instance, the book that seemed so promising ended up on my bookshelf, gathering dust. I can assure you, it is not our intention that this book end up in your bookcase, filled with promise, but unable to deliver.

There are three simple rules that need to be followed in order to use this book with a measure of satisfaction.

Place: It is important that you choose a place for reading that provides the necessary atmosphere for reflection and that does not allow for too many distractions. Whatever place you choose needs to be comfortable, have the necessary lighting, and, finally, have a sense of "welcoming" about it. You need to be able to look forward to the experience of the journey. Don't travel steerage if you know you will be more comfortable in first class and if the choice is realistic for you. On the other hand, if first class is a distraction and you feel more comfortable and more yourself in steerage, then it is in steerage that you belong.

My favorite place is an overstuffed and comfortable chair in my bedroom. There is a light over my shoulder, and the chair reclines if I feel a need to recline. Once in a while, I get lucky and the sun comes through my window and bathes the entire room in light. I have other options and other places that are available to me but this is the place that I prefer.

Time: Choose a time during the day when you are most alert and when you are most receptive to reflection, meditation, and prayer. The time that you choose is an essential component. If you are a morning person, for example, you should choose a time that is in the morning. If you are more alert in the afternoon, choose an afternoon time slot; and if evening is your preference, then by all means choose the evening. Try to avoid "peak" periods in your daily routine when you know that you might be disturbed. The time that you choose needs to be your time and needs to work for you.

It is also important that you choose how much time you will spend with your companion each day. For some it will be possible to set aside enough time in order to read and reflect on all the material that is offered for a given day. For others, it might not be possible to devote one time to the suggested material for the day, so the prayer period may need to be extended for two, three, or even more sessions. It is not important how long it takes you; it is only important that it works for you and that you remain committed to that which is possible.

For myself I have found that fifteen minutes in the early morning, while I am still in my robe and pajamas and before my morning coffee, and even before I prepare myself for the day, is the best time. No one expects to see me or to interact with me because I have not yet "announced" the fact that I am awake or even on the move. However, once someone hears me in the bathroom, then my window of opportunity is gone. It is therefore important to me that I use the time that I have identified when it is available to me.

Freedom: It may seem strange to suggest that freedom is the third necessary ingredient, but I have discovered that it is most important. By freedom I understand a certain "stance toward life," a "permission to be myself and to be gentle and understanding of who I am." I am constantly amazed at how the human person so easily sets himself or herself up for disappointment and perceived failure. We so easily make judgments about ourselves and our actions and our choices, and very often those judgments are negative, and not at all helpful.

For instance, what does it really matter if I have chosen a place and a time, and I have missed both the place and the time for three days in a row? What does it matter if I have chosen, in that twilight time before I am completely awake and still a little sleepy, to roll over and to sleep for fifteen minutes more? Does it mean that I am not serious about the journey, that I really don't want to pray, that I am just fooling myself when I say that my prayer time is important to me? Perhaps, but I prefer to believe that it simply means that I am tired and I just wanted a little more sleep. It doesn't mean anything more than that. However, if I make it mean more than that, then I can become discouraged, frustrated, and put myself into a state where I might more easily give up. "What's the use? I might as well forget all about it."

The same sense of freedom applies to the reading and the praying of this text. If I do not find the introduction to each day helpful, I don't need to read it. If I find the questions for reflection at the end of the appointed day repetitive, then I should choose to close the book and go my own way. Even if I discover that the reflection offered for the day is not the one that I prefer and that the one for the next day seems more inviting, then by all means, go on to the one for the next day.

That's it! If you apply these simple rules to your journey you should receive the maximum benefit and you will soon find yourself at your destination. But be prepared to be surprised. If you have never been on a spiritual journey you should know that the "travel brochures" and the other descriptions that you might have heard are nothing compared to the real thing. There is so much more than you can imagine.

A final prayer of blessing suggests itself:

Lord, catch me off guard today. Surprise me
with some moment of
      beauty or pain
So that at least for the moment
I may be startled into seeing that you
   are here in all your splendor,
Always and everywhere,
Barely hidden,
Beneath,
Beyond,
Within this life I breathe.

Frederick Buechner

Rev. Thomas M. Santa, CSsR
Liguori, Missouri

Henri Nouwen's Chronology

1932   Born in Nijkerk, Holland (January 24)

1957   Ordained to the Roman Catholic priesthood in the archdiocese of Utrecht, Holland

1957–64   Student in psychology at the Catholic University of Nijmegen, Holland

1964–66   Fellow in the program for religion and psychiatry at the Menninger Foundation, Topeka, Kansas

1968–70   Staff Member of the Pastoral Institute, Amsterdam, Holland, and faculty member of the Catholic Theological Institute, Utrecht, Holland

1970–71   Student of Theological Studies, University of Nijmegen, Holland

1971–77   Associate Professor of Pastoral Theology, Yale Divinity School, New Haven, Connecticut

1974	Received Tenure at Yale
1974	Six months at the Abbey of Genesee, Piffard, up-state New York
1976	Fellow at the Ecumenical Institute, Collegeville, Minnesota
1977–81	Professor of Pastoral Theology, Yale Divinity School, New Haven, Connecticut
1978	Scholar-in-residence, New American College, Rome
1979	Six month stay at the Abbey of Genesee
1981–82	Six month stay in Bolivia and Peru
1983–85	Professor and lecturer, Harvard Divinity School
1985–86	Nine month residence, L'Arche, Trosly-Breuil, France
1986–96	Pastor, L'Arche Daybreak, Richmond Hill, Ontario, Canada
1996	Died on September 21 in Hilvesum, Holland, age sixty-four

A Few Notes on
Henri Nouwen

*D*uring late twentieth century two important spiritual masters emerged: Thomas Merton and Henri Nouwen. Nouwen is still read by hundreds of thousands, if not millions, of Catholics and Christians of other denominations.

Nouwen was a new, modern kind of priest. He did not just want to proselytize but to search for a deeper understanding of people, of their inner conflicts and of their fears. In short, he sought to understand their woundedness and to find ways to cure them. Unlike many of his contemporary priests who suspected it, he took a great interest in psychology. Foreseeing the future trend of a marriage between psychology and spirituality in pastoral ministry, he applied for and received a fellowship in the program for religion and psychiatry at the Menninger Foundation, Topeka, Kansas.

Nouwen studied psychology because at root he recognized his own woundedness. As a priest, he had developed acute powers of self-examination; thus, he understood himself, discerned his flaws, recognized his psychological wounds. He came to realize that if he could find therapeutic ways to help himself with his own personal neuroses, he might be able to help others. This desire to help others propelled him into a new, exciting kind of ministry: priest as *The Wounded Healer*, the title of his groundbreaking book that is still in print and is required in many college courses and in most seminaries.

During the cultural revolution of the 1960s, when Nouwen arrived from Holland, young Americans were questioning everything, especially their country's involvement in the Vietnam War. They challenged not only their leaders' values but also the values of their parents and churches. At heart, they were seeking truth. Nouwen, himself a seeker, entered into the quest of these young people through his professorships at Notre Dame, Yale Divinity School and Harvard Divinity School.

It was clear to him that young people were searching for a deeper spiritual life. Like the Beatles and other prominent cultural figures many were turning to the East for answers. Nouwen, however, offered his students Jesus Christ of the New Testament, his primary goal in pastoral ministry, to return them home to the man of sorrows who offers healing to those seeking wholeness of soul and psyche.

This gifted, charismatic teacher found his classes overflowing with students attracted to a professor who spoke from his own experience. He was interested in helping them establish an intimate relationship with Christ. He spoke as if Christ were his close personal friend — which indeed was true because he was a man of deep, faithful prayer. Students' praise of Nouwen as a teacher and Christian spread from the classroom to the general public; he later reached a wider audience through his best-selling books. Before long Nouwen became an iconic spiritual leader.

To reach as many people as he could, he held campus social hours where students of different ages, genders, backgrounds, and religions discussed the real, heart-piercing, often controversial issues that affected their lives. At the center stood Nouwen, born and raised in Holland, a man for whom English was a second language, a man reaching out to as many people as he could about the good news of the Gospel. His books grew out of his pastoral ministry.

Why, so many years after his death, are Nouwen's books still popular? His writing is direct, lucid, and heartfelt. Although an academic, Nouwen understood that to touch the spiritual core of real people, those who struggled every day to make ends meet as well as those more fortunate, he had to connect with them.

To this end, he wrote in a style that anyone could understand. He used plain language and simple sentences; above all, he shared his innermost self: he placed no intermediary mask between him and his readers, no talking down to them, no jargon, no holier than thou attitude — only a humble solidarity. He, like them, was seeking a deeper communion with our Lord.

Reading Nouwen, people saw themselves. He may have been a distinguished professor, a highly educated intellectual from an upper class background, but he knew how to communicate with people from every station in life. His message was simple: "I'm on a journey too. I too seek inner peace. I too seek healing. Let's take this journey together, for I promise you that in the end we will find the peace that passes understanding."

The sales figures for his books suggest that countless people have taken the journey with Henri Nouwen. His rise as a spiritual force in both the English and the non-English speaking world is not fully appreciated. In the latter part of the twentieth century, the best-selling spiritual writers were Thomas Merton, Thomas Moore, Kathleen Norris and Henri Nouwen. Nouwen, a gifted preacher, was invited everywhere. He spoke at universities and churches, even on television's Hour of Power from the

Crystal Cathedral, where he delivered one of his most powerful and moving homilies.

Nouwen's spiritual influence continues in the twenty-first century. Why do so many still seek him as a spiritual master? The appeal of any one author to such a wide spectrum of nationalities, languages, religions, genders and ages defies easy explanation. No one can predict what books will be bestsellers, what plays will be hits, what movies will become classics, what poems might transform lives. They all share one thing, however: they somehow shed light on the human condition, offering hope.

Nouwen offers a spirituality that anyone can practice, a spirituality without a smidgen of the esoteric or the enigmatic or the tag of "only for proficients" or "only for the holy." His spirituality says, "You do not have to be a cloistered nun or monk. You do not have to be a priest. You do not have to be a person of rare holiness or even a very good person to stand before and reach out to Christ." His spirituality exclaims for all to hear: God accepts and loves you *as you are now*, with all your imperfections, flaws, and wounds.

The word "sin" rarely shows up in Nouwen's works. People do not respond to fire and brimstone sermons. Most realize their sins full well. Nouwen understood that "sin" is often the result of wounds. We cannot eliminate the painful roots that extend from childhood into the rest of life. Thus, Nouwen teaches that the first stage of the spiritual journey, the *sine qua non* of the spiritual life, is self-forgiveness and self-acceptance. Without learning to love ourselves, he warns, we cannot love our brothers and sisters, and we cannot love God. His message actually is not new: it is the message of Jesus Christ.

The very heart of Nouwen's spirituality lies in Christ's parable of the Prodigal Son. This parable that so moved Nouwen exhorts us to return home to God, no questions asked, no "mea culpa" necessary — even if you are dressed in rags, even if you smell of the pigs you fed, even if you have squandered your inheritance — just come home to a Father who will embrace you with joy and love, restoring you to the status as a beloved daughter or son that you never lost.

Scholars are investigating Nouwen's extraordinary life and spiritual message. Wil Hernandez, for instance, is exploring Nouwen's modern approach to spiritual formation in *Henri Nouwen, A Spirituality of Imperfection.*

The word "imperfection" alone summarizes Nouwen's outlook concerning the contemporary search for meaning. He encourages us to embrace our imperfection and to offer it as our unique gift to God who alone, like the Father in the parable of the Prodigal Son, can transform woundedness and imperfection. No matter how imperfect we are, he loves us with an agapetic love, no strings attached except, perhaps, for the golden thread used only to lead us back to him.

At his death, Henri Nouwen left a number of golden threads: his books. Each, if read attentively, will lead us back into to God's loving embrace. I can think of no greater legacy: to help every son and daughter return to their loving Father.

Introduction

I first encountered Henri Nouwen at St. Paul's Church in Cambridge, Massachusetts. At the time he was teaching at Harvard College, and St. Paul's had invited him. I had been advised he was an eloquent speaker on the spiritual life and should not miss the opportunity to hear him.

I was fortunate to find a seat in the packed hall. He was, indeed, a dynamic preacher. I shall never forget his huge hands gesticulating as he emphasized a point, and his voice, particularly his Dutch accent, which added a certain charm. I also recall the utter seriousness of his message: a call for a closer, more intimate relationship with Christ.

To this day I wish I had taken notes. My impression of him was thoroughly positive: his was an authentic spiritual voice that ranked alongside my other spiritual mentor, Thomas Merton. There was, however, a definite difference between the two. Merton appealed to the intellect, but Nouwen appealed to the heart; he understood that the hunger for God resides not in the mind, but the heart — as enunciated in the fourteenth-century treatise *The Cloud of Unknowing*: "God cannot be reached through the intellect and by reason but through love."

Unlike Merton, who was a Catholic apologist, Nouwen was less concerned about theology and more interested in spirituality. Thus, he led people to God not through mystical abstraction but through the intimacy of his personal relationship with Christ. This is why he opened his heart to his audience, sharing the details of his spiritual journey, its ups and downs. His listeners and readers were moved, if not charmed, by his willingness to be himself — to step down from the priestly pedestal of authority to talk with each of us, heart-to-heart.

During his youth in Holland, when most boys were happily playing cowboy and Indians or war games, Nouwen's favorite pastime was to playact as a priest. Observing his inclination, his grandmother ordered vestments to be made and a small altar built for him in the attic; his brother often served as his acolyte while his childhood friends played along as if they were attending Mass.

It was evident early on that Nouwen was destined to become a priest. It is not surprising because he came from a religious family, his mother and father being devout Catholics. He also had an aunt who was a nun, and his uncle Anton was a well-known priest in Holland.

After ordination, Nouwen refused to be put on a pedestal. He walked in solidarity among the faithful in order to understand their anguish, their anxieties, their fears and their wounds. Above all he wanted to help them, not just preach or remind them of their sinfulness.

Because of his ability to embrace and share his own woundedness, he learned that he had the gift of helping the wounded. At that time, it was unusual for a priest to reveal his vulnerability so openly. And people took notice.

He understood that "nuclear man" had suffered a break with the past and with the symbols that once nourished him. He clearly saw that existential anxiety left people anguished, fragmented, apathetic, and confused. He understood Carl Jung's wisdom: modern men and women were searching for their souls, for the source of being and the reality of the unseen. In short, they sought God, although many did not understand what they were searching for. They were truly lost souls.

In his ground-breaking *The Wounded Healer,* Nouwen states his belief that in order to serve his fellow Christians, he had to admit and reveal his own wounds. Too often priests remained aloof, presenting themselves as experts with quick, facile answers to life's dilemmas, answers that were merely theoretical (and thus of little value), not experiential. Nouwen, however, perceived that modern life was complicated for Christians; he also confessed to the same kinds of fears and wounds his flock experienced — he too was often lonely and unhappy; he too suffered from anxiety, depression, from feelings of self-rejection, inferiority and unworthiness.

His revolutionary message began with a recognition of our wounds, followed by their acceptance and integration. Only then will we find healing through that greatest of revolutionaries, Jesus Christ, who accepts and loves us as we are. To follow Jesus' example is to love ourselves, for only when we accept and love ourselves can we accept and love others.

From his mother, he learned that what is most personal is also universal. Like that great articulator of American thinking, Ralph Waldo Emerson, Nouwen understood that those who understand themselves also understand other people. All men and women constitute a single family; hence, our problems are universal. Thus, through his own self-acceptance, Nouwen attained a profound empathy and compassion, helping him to reach out to multitudes.

At Notre Dame, Yale and Harvard he taught to standing room only crowds. Young people, in particular, flocked to his classes because the Christianity he spoke of reached across political, social and religious barriers, excluding no one. His message was deceptively simple: The answers to life's problems lie within you, within your own house (self), within the center of your heart where Christ abides (Christ is our True Self).

Most would have found teaching at Harvard the pinnacle of success. Nouwen, however, abandoned his illustrious academic career to live among the handicapped at Daybreak, a L'Arche community founded by Jean Vanier outside Toronto, Canada. Life at Daybreak was the antithesis of life at Harvard. No one knew of his fame as a speaker and writer, nor could they read or understand his books. They simply considered him their pastor.

He was assigned to care for a severely handicapped young man named Adam. At first, bathing, dressing and caring of Adam taxed Nouwen's patience; in the morning he was usually anxious about beginning work at his office. Adam slowed him down and taught him a spirituality of waiting, of weakness, of silence, forever transforming Nouwen's life. Adam's death devastated Nouwen, who admitted that more than anyone he had ever met, Adam had connected him most with God.

In the end, however, even Adam could not slow Henri Nouwen down. His great tension and energy drove him to reach as many people as he could through his writing and speaking. His frenetic lifestyle finally caught up with him in 1996, when a heart attack took from contemporary Christianity one of its greatest spiritual voices.

We who remain are most fortunate because Nouwen was prolific, having written over forty books. His is a tremendous, spiritually empowering legacy, one we can turn to time and time again, especially when we need to hear the saving word, when we need someone to speak to us heart-to-heart, to remind us that Christ is present, ever ready to assist us, to forgive us, to accept us, to love us — his love being eternal and agapetic: unconditional.

1
Agape

Focus Point

////////////

Christians often take God's love for granted. They really should ask, "Do we really believe in God's unconditional love for each of us?" Ponder this: God loves us unconditionally. What does this mean? No matter what we do, no matter how many times we fail, God loves us. He accepts us as we are. Fr. Nouwen believed in God's unconditional love. Without it, he would not have survived even a day in his hectic life as a priest, preacher and pastor.

////////////

God's love for us existed before we were born and will exist after we have died.

(*Bread for the Journey*,
February 5)

////////////

*J*esus Christ's Parable of the Prodigal Son had always been Nouwen's favorite. Its true message, however, did not hit home until he encountered Rembrandt's famous painting. In fact, it was not the actual painting that first caught his attention, but a huge poster of it. Nouwen so loved Rembrandt's masterpiece he later traveled to the Hermitage Museum, St. Petersburg, Russia, to view it, a visit that resulted in a book. The painting had pierced his heart, leaving upon it an indelible mark.

The book Nouwen wrote in response, *The Return of the Prodigal Son*, became one of his most popular. The painting depicts the father embracing one bedraggled son, while to the father's left his elder son, aloof and judgmental, stares at the two of them. At first, Nouwen identified with the son who dissipated his inheritance and ended up feeding pigs who ate better than he did. Nouwen had had a troubled relationship with his father who, he was convinced, considered him a failure, but this supposition was not based on fact but on Nouwen's feelings of insecurity regarding his father's approval of him. Such negative feelings about himself were not rare for Nouwen; he was often filled with self-doubt. It rendered him so needy that he made great demands upon his friends for approval, acceptance and affection, often annoying, if not distancing, many of them.

His mother raised him according to a book that warned parents not to "spoil" their babies with too much attention and touch. By following the book's advice and techniques, she unfortunately caused her son for much of his life to crave the touch his mother had denied him. Realizing her mistake, she later apologized for the damage she had inadvertently done.

He also identified with the elder son because he was the eldest of four children. In the painting the elder son looks mystified by his father's poignant expression of love for a son who threw away his inheritance, who abandoned his father, who lived the life of a libertine. We can imagine the older brother thinking, "Why has my father never expressed his love for me?" He is simultaneously hurt and resentful.

Unlike his brothers, Nouwen did not achieve material success. Because he worked in God's vineyards, he did not have many worldly trophies to show off to his father. He did find academic success and published many books, but such honors did not quiet Nouwen's longing to hear praise and admiration from his father's lips.

A friend suggested to Nouwen that he ought to identify not with the sons in Rembrandt's painting, but with the father. As a priest Nouwen was a *pater*, a father to his flock. The comment opened his eyes and transformed his life.

The theme of the painting is Unconditional Love, Agape. The son tries to pronounce his "mea culpa," but the father lets that pass, instead calling his servants to wash him, replace his rags with robes, place a ring on his finger and sandals on his feet. He decides to celebrate the son who was "dead" but has again come to life. Such is God's love for each of us: He rejoices when we return to him. Like the father in the parable, God does not ask for explanations. And no matter how many times we stray, he will always rejoice at our return.

The parable of the Prodigal Son can resonate with each of us. We all have been prodigals, but God is always present, eagerly awaiting our return home.

Nouwen himself resembled the "prodigal" son in that after living in America for many years, he had returned to his native land when the fatal heart attack struck. He had arrived in Holland with the intention of continuing on for his second visit to the Hermitage Museum to film a documentary about Rembrandt's *The Return of the Prodigal Son*, a project dear to his heart.

Reflection Questions

Which son am I like — the prodigal or the elder? Do I accept God's unconditional love or do I, like the elder son, question and doubt it? Have I embraced the Father? Have I embraced Agape? Have I expressed agapetic love in my life, particularly to my friends, to my relatives, to my spouse, to my children?

2
Intimacy

Focus Point

////////////

We all long for intimacy; thus, many yearn for a happy marriage. Nouwen believed, however, that in our lives we have Two Loves. The First Love is for God. Then follow all others. God is closer than we are to ourselves: nothing is more intimate than God's love.

////////////

Today the struggle for intimacy is no longer limited to one age group. In the midst of a competitive and demanding world, people of all ages have become painfully aware of their deep-seated desire for a place of intimacy.

(*Intimacy*, p. 2)

////////////

*T*he word intimate derives from the Latin word *intimus,* meaning "innermost." In anatomy, the intima is the innermost layer of an organ. To become intimate with others we must open ourselves so as to reveal our innermost selves.

Intimacy, therefore, is based on being and sharing our true selves with one another, hiding behind no masks. It is easier to be intimate with God, for he knows every crook and corner of our mind and soul. We can hide nothing from him. He knows us better than we know ourselves, and if we are willing to turn to God, to offer him space in our lives, to pray daily, we can establish an intimate relationship.

Intimacy does not arrive naturally; we must work for it. By doing so, we allow God to divine (that is, define) us; thus, the search for meaning in our lives, to borrow Victor Frankl's expression, is fulfilled.

To become intimate with people, we risk being hurt; consequently, we often wear personae (masks) to camouflage our real selves, but when we become comfortable (and safe) wearing them, we fail to connect with others on an intimate level; our relationships are, therefore, superficial.

It is natural to fear being hurt by others, knowing full well that in sundry ways the world is a hostile, competitive place. Christ himself warns us to be on guard in the world: to be as gentle as doves yet wise as serpents. Thus, to allow ourselves to be vulnerable (the Latin word *vulnus* means "wound") demands courage, for we never know when another may inadvertently or deliberately wound us. As few of us escape it, being prepared for wounding is our best defense.

Fr. Nouwen counsels us not only to open ourselves to others; in fact, he is far more daring. He says, like Christ, that we must love one another unconditionally, even when another wounds us. Loving does not mean only listening to or tolerating others; it means a mutuality of acceptance — with no strings attached. It is as if we are saying to another, "Your strengths are my strengths and your weaknesses are my weaknesses."

Nouwen lived his life this way. He loved people, and because he loved them, he was willing to share with them his whole self. This is one of the many reasons why so many read his books: they are deeply moved because Nouwen seems to be speaking directly to them about their personal problems, which are in essence the same ones he had to face and to solve.

It is not difficult to get to know Henri Nouwen. He is maskless, hiding nothing. He does not just intimate things about himself but openly shares his whole self. His diaries reveal a person just like

ourselves, through his unashamed record of
every emotion, be it envy, anger, joy, or fear.
When he faces problems with other people he
works them out, his writing serving as therapy,
helping him to zero in on the cause of his
dilemmas.

Nouwen encourages us to keep an inner
corner of ourselves for God alone, what the
Quaker Thomas Kelly calls the *Shekinah* of
the soul. We have within us an inner sanctuary
where we can meet with God at any moment.
Time must be set aside for prayer, but prayers
can also be offered throughout the day. Whether
driving a car or riding on a train or working we
can still take a moment to remember God. In a
swift turning of our mind to God, we can thank
and praise him. Such efforts will surely affect
the quality of our days, adding to them a holy
intimacy. It takes only a second to offer God
small prayers, like the Jesus Prayer. Such brief
moments keep us intimate with our Lord.

Nouwen left Harvard because, although he
was encouraging everyone to pray more, he
found himself too busy teaching, writing and
preaching to pray. At that time he decided to
become the pastor at Daybreak.

Reflection Questions

Do I really want intimacy with God? Or am I afraid because intimacy means I must live according to God's will? Am I willing to surrender my mind, body and soul to God? Am I willing to surrender my will to God's? In short, am I willing to embrace divine intimacy and emulate Christ in all things?

3
The Circus

Focus Point

////////////

One of the most difficult aspects of the spiritual life is surrendering to God's will. Thus, the greatest prayer we can ever utter is Jesus', "Not my will but yours be done" (Lk 22:42). Nouwen offered his life to God, and in every major decision of his life he prayed to be shown God's will. When he perceived what God wanted of him, he dropped everything to follow.

////////////

Lord, open my hands to receive your gift of love.
(*With Open Hands*, p. 61)

////////////

*M*any of Nouwen's books have covers illustrated with paintings by the twentieth century Catholic master artist, Georges Rouault (1871–1958). Deeply moved by the Shroud of Turin, Rouault often painted the iconic *sainte face* (holy face) of Christ, the man of sorrows, as well as those of circus clowns. He understood that the clown's mask often concealed a man of sorrow who lived a nomadic life full of uncertainty and pain. Like the clowns he painted, Rouault too had suffered, but wore a mask of cheerfulness to spare others his pain.

Having retained his childlike sense of wonder, Nouwen was fascinated by the circus, particularly clowns and trapeze artists. In Jungian terms, he was a *puer aeternus,* an "eternal boy." Such an adult maintains childlike, unworldly virtues of innocence and the ability to appreciate marvels with which most adults have long lost touch.

The clowns who particularly moved Nouwen are marginal persons who cause people to laugh because they appear absurd and out of step. Some might consider clowning useless, but to Nouwen it served a purpose: to remind us not to take ourselves too seriously. Clowns also remind us to find humor in our life; by doing so, our preoccupations, worries, tensions and anxieties need not overcome us. Every person is called to put on a white face and a huge painted smile.

The clown serves as a reminder that even when life seems fraught with "quiet desperation," we can still smile and even laugh. A sense of humor can sustain a person through a difficult time. The clown also personifies solitude. Each person is alone. Each must face what life presents. Rather than fleeing solitude, we must learn to embrace it.

In solitude we find our true self. In solitude we find strength and discover the eternal verities. Most importantly, in solitude we become aware of the One who is the center of our very being, Christ.

Many fear solitude. They seek comfort in other people and activity. Doing so, however, serves as an escape from facing ourselves, from getting to know ourselves, from getting to know God. The best way to become intimate with God is simple surrender to him: "Not my will but yours be done."

This is what trapeze artists do. They make flying seem elegant and miraculous. Trapeze acts thrill children, but they can also thrill adults who can let their inner child be captivated by the sight before them. These artists so thrilled Nouwen that he befriended the famous European Rodleigh family troupe. Enchanted by his open, unaffected friendliness, they took him into their family. Their mutual love moved Nouwen, who discerned a spiritual dimension in their circus act. At first amazed by the person who, suspended in mid-air, flies alone above the ground, he came to realize that the most important person in the act is not the flier, but the catcher. Because the Rodleighs worked without a net, the flier would otherwise have fallen to certain death.

Nouwen saw a spiritual philosophy in the utter importance of the catcher, a reminder that in our spiritual lives we are fortunate to have a God who is always there to catch us whenever we are about to "fall."

Nouwen died before he could write a book about this spiritual trapeze way of living. But he had already written many other books that we can turn to in troubled times, books that serve us as "catchers," preventing our fall into depression, into self-rejection, anxiety and fear. Although he may not have consciously chosen to serve this role, through God's grace Nouwen has become a catcher of souls, his trapeze "act" still appreciated by countless people.

Reflection Questions

Am I willing to be a clown for Christ? Am I willing to become one of his fools, knowing full well that many look askance at committed Christians? Am I willing to stand up for my faith when it flies in the face of popular opinion? Am I courageous enough to practice my faith and support its precepts? Am I willing to allow God be the catcher in my life?

4
Van Gogh

Focus Point

////////////

Henri Nouwen felt a great attraction to the visual arts, particularly paintings by his countrymen van Gogh and Rembrandt. Like Fr. Nouwen, we all should recall that the source of all beauty is God. God uses beauty, Simone Weil says, as a snare to lure us to him. Nouwen willingly allowed himself to be a "victim" to God's snare.

////////////

Although Vincent van Gogh is certainly not a religious writer in the traditional sense of the word, for me he was a man whose spirit touched my spirit very deeply, and who brought me in touch with some aspects of the spiritual life that no formal writer ever did.

(Quoted by Michael Ford in *Wounded Prophet,*
A Portrait of Henri J. Nouwen, p. 10)

////////////

*R*embrandt and van Gogh suffered immensely, but were able to transcend their pain by creating inimitable art.

The letters between Vincent and his brother Theo moved Nouwen deeply. Vincent's love for his brother leaps off the page. His early letters reveal the young Vincent, very much in love with Christ, devoted to spreading the good news of the Gospel. He was also profoundly moved by the lives of those barely able to eke out an existence, as illustrated in his haunting *The Potato Eaters.*

Few know that van Gogh first felt called to be a minister. In England he served at several Methodist schools and churches, giving his first sermon in 1876 at a little church in Richmond. He sent his brother a copy with the note, "It is a delightful thought that in the future, wherever I go, I shall preach the Gospel; to do that well, one must have the Gospel in one's heart. May the Lord give it to me."[1]

Nouwen's seminar on "The Ministry of Vincent van Gogh" was one of the most popular courses at Yale Divinity School. He created a one-man show, playing the great artist himself. Nouwen felt a great affinity with van Gogh, a wounded and broken genius wracked by fear and insecurity. Van Gogh helped Nouwen realize his own brokenness. Like van Gogh, Nouwen desired to spread the Gospel, but unlike van Gogh, he succeeded because he found creative ways to reach his students. Nouwen understood that even though van Gogh had failed as a preacher, he was a born artist, faithful to his True Self. Once Nouwen came to understand that his own True Self lay in teaching, preaching and writing, he set himself to developing completely the gifts God had given him.

Vincent van Gogh sought to help people see and live in a new, life-transforming way. He hoped that his paintings would open not only eyes but also hearts. Although lacking the theological training of a minister, van Gogh was indeed God's messenger, encouraging his viewers to cleanse their doors of perception and to embrace *metanoia*, a change of heart. Only by doing so can the beauty of the world, of people, of God become visible.

Great art, therefore, generates a new way of seeing. An artist and a priest share the same purpose: to teach others to see God in nature, in people, and in art. To develop this new vision, Nouwen himself had to become an "artist." He honed his skills as a preacher and actor. His portrayal of Vincent van Gogh became one of his most successful ministries.

Although a born writer, Nouwen worked to develop his communication skills. His greatest gifts were simplicity and transparency. Readers saw themselves in Nouwen because he shared with them his own vulnerability. This was a revolutionary kind of spiritual writing. Fulton Sheen, although a gifted spiritual writer and orator, never became intimate with his audience. Unlike Sheen, Nouwen became a companion along their spiritual journey.

In his eloquent foreword to Cliff Edwards' *van Gogh and God, A Creative Spiritual Quest,* Nouwen writes, "He painted what I had not before dared to look at; he questioned what I had not before dared to speak about; and he entered into spaces of the heart that I had not before dared to come close to. By doing so he brought me further and deeper in my search for a God who loves."[2]

What van Gogh did for Nouwen, Nouwen continues to accomplish for modern readers. Reading can be a spiritual way. A paragraph, a sentence, even a word can transform a life. Amidst our radios, televisions, cell phones, iPods, and computers, we should set time aside to read. A book can touch, can even heal a wound, returning a reader to a full life. Books like those of Henri Nouwen can return us to God.

Reflection Questions

Have I opened my eyes to God's beauty in the world? Have I taken time to visit museums and feast my eyes upon the great masterpieces of art? Have I pondered the lesson of beauty, that if the beauty of the entire world could be taken in by a glance, it could never equal the beauty of God, the source of all beauty? Is my life beautiful? Am I following my vocation, to be an artist of my life, creating a beauty by emulating the life of Christ?

5
Monasticism

Focus Point

////////////

Monastic life, which requires sacrificing the beauty of marriage and family for total devotion to the contemplation of God Alone, is not for most people. Nouwen, a celibate priest, led a difficult life; when it became too arduous, he went to monasteries to be spiritually renewed and invigorated.

////////////

Contemplative life is a human response to the fundamental fact that the central things in life, although spiritually perceptible, remain invisible in large measure and can very easily be overlooked by the inattentive, busy, distracted person that each of us can so readily become.

(*Genesee Diary,*
Report from a Trappist Monastery, p. 36)

//////////////

*T*homas Merton's books on spirituality and his way of life as a Trappist monk fascinated Nouwen. In fact, he tried to emulate Merton's monastic way of life, living at Genesee Abbey in upstate New York for two six-month periods. Nouwen accepted Merton's spiritual counsel about the need for silence and solitude in our modern, frenetic lives. We cannot hear the "still, small voice" of God if we are constantly bombarded with noise and overwhelmed by activity. Nouwen had to face that particular dilemma because of his whirlwind of teaching, preaching and writing.

Thus, in 1974 and again in 1979, Nouwen left the world for Genesee Abbey where he embraced a Trappist monk's life of *ora et labora*, prayer and work. Like Merton, he often wrote about the need for more prayer in our lives, for more solitude and silence in the hope of an encounter with God. But he was so busy writing books, lecturing, accepting speaking engagements, and traveling that he himself failed to practice what he preached.

Because the Trappists are one of the strictest Catholic religious orders, it is extraordinary that Nouwen was allowed to live at Genesee as one of the community of monks. Abbot John Eudes Bamburger requested that his community allow Nouwen to live among them and to follow the Rule of St. Benedict. They agreed to Nouwen's temporary admission. Thomas Merton had been Bamburger's spiritual director, and he now served as Nouwen's counselor, an extraordinary linkage for Nouwen, who had met Merton only once.

At first, Nouwen found it difficult to slow down. To a man always on the go, the pace at Genesee was the antithesis of his accustomed life. Consequently, he had problems adjusting to living as a monk. He was awkward, and helping the monks make bread (their way of supporting themselves) was often a tale of bumbling mishaps. Although physically weak, he helped the monks build their new chapel, requiring him to move huge stones, a hardship for an academic who had never lifted anything heavier than a book.

His real purpose for going to Genesee was to pray, but again his prayer life was disrupted by his life-long emotional problems: an inordinate need for affection and affirmation, a need for people and their attention, a need for activity, in brief, a need to be needed. Although he loved the peace, order and structure of Genesee, as well as its natural beauty, it was actually too peaceful, too lonely and too structured for him.

Nouwen, an inveterate writer, maintained a detailed diary of his time at Genesee. He poured his heart into it: the difficulties, mishaps, frustration, anxiety, and his struggles with prayer. It quickly became a bestseller and catapulted him into the front ranks of spiritual writers.

Journaling was Nouwen's forte. His journals are riveting because he keeps nothing back; he stands before his readers in all his vulnerability, unlike Merton's precisely crafted works in which the author rarely unmasks himself, careful not to mar the pious, near saintly, monastic image readers had of him.

Genesee Diary conveys the portrait of a flawed, endearing, awkward and occasionally comical man. And readers love and admire him for it. He reaches out to ordinary people with similar and sometimes foolish, even clownish flaws, with a clear message: You can have an intimate relationship with God by being yourself, warts and all.

Henri Nouwen and Abbot Bamburger had one serious disagreement, concerning who could receive the Holy Eucharist at Mass. When Nouwen celebrated his twenty-fifth anniversary as a priest, he invited 150 family members and friends to Genesse to celebrate it with him. Many of his friends were non-Catholic, and Nouwen had customarily distributed the Eucharist to all his friends who approached him.

Bamburger insisted that Nouwen follow the Church's dictum that only practicing Catholics were to receive the Eucharist. Although displeased, Nouwen obeyed. His usual practice, however, suggests the kind of man and priest he was: he saw Christ in everyone; thus, he felt that he should not deny anyone the Eucharist, but at Genesee he obeyed Bamburger, who once described a monk as a man who wants to be ruled by an abbot.

At a monastery, lay people can get away from the world's "getting and spending" and freely be by themselves in the silence and solitude. In such a holy place they can gain a greater perspective of their lives. And if they use the time well, particularly by devoting more of it to prayer, they can also move closer to our Lord.

Most monasteries offer weekend or week retreats. Participants are usually asked to pay only what they can afford. What they receive from their stay, however, is priceless, and may transform their lives forever.

Reflection Questions

Have I made room for silence and solitude in my life? Have I cultivated a monastic cell within my soul where I can commune with the Christ abiding in me? Have I tried to receive the Eucharist as often as possible? Have I made my heart *hospitable*, as Nouwen would say, for Christ?

6
Home

Focus Point

////////////

When Nouwen came to America, he lived a nomadic life, going from one university to another. He seemingly lived out of a suitcase. When Jean Vanier invited him to Daybreak, he actually found a home. During his close study of Rembrandt's *The Return of the Prodigal Son*, he also realized that our true home is Christ: "Abide in me as I abide in you" (Jn 15:4).

////////////

When I first saw Rembrandt's painting, I was not as familiar with the home of God within me, as I am now.... I was desperately searching for that inner place where I too could be held as safely as the young man in the painting.

(*The Return of the Prodigal Son*, p. 17)

////////////

*L*ike Thomas Merton, for a long time Nouwen was homeless. Merton finally found a home at the Abbey of Gethsemani in Kentucky, with the added boon that the Gethsemani monks also became his family. Nouwen, however, found it more difficult to find a place he could call his home, a community he could call family.

He did not find it at Notre Dame, Yale and Harvard. Each professorship offered him something desirable, either control over his curriculum or having semesters off so that he could write his books. What he really wanted, however, was a place where he could be himself and feel at ease being himself.

Teaching at Harvard, most would agree, would be the zenith of anyone's career. It seemed that he had everything: popularity with his students and packed classes where he spoke eloquently about the spiritual life, about establishing a close relationship with Jesus Christ. But Nouwen was not happy there.

He made Christ come alive, as if he were actually present. He could speak as he did because he believed in the eternal Jesus ever present in the Now. He spoke not as a theologian but as a man of faith, who based his life on Jesus and His teachings. To him, Jesus was not an abstraction, a figure in abstruse theological books perused in dusty libraries and later discussed at round intellectual tables. For him, Jesus was real: he was born in this world of a mother, he walked the earth, he ate, he slept, he had friends, he gazed upon the beauty of the world. He loved the poor and homeless, and entered into the sorrow of the world. A real man, he was at the same time divine. Nouwen believed this with his whole heart, mind and soul, and he shared his belief with everyone he ever met.

At Harvard, God was spoken of theoretically and in hushed, if not embarrassed, tones. "Preaching" was unseemly. No one else spoke about intimacy with Jesus as Nouwen often did. Thus, Nouwen embarrassed; many of his Harvard colleagues considered him politically incorrect. Of course, Nouwen was Catholic, and Catholics had traditionally been viewed with suspicion there. The autobiography of George Santayana reveals the religious bias that dominated Harvard during the latter part of the nineteenth century. It still lingered there when Nouwen arrived in the latter part of the twentieth century. He did not need such tension, but a place of security, peace and acceptance.

Jean Vanier, who had founded the L'Arche communities in 1964, invited Nouwen to Trosly-Breuil, an hour from Paris. He said, "Maybe we can offer you a home here." Although Nouwen loved Trosly and established close friendships with Vanier's mother and Thomas Phillipe, co-founder of L'Arche, it would not be his final home.

In October of 1985, during a visit to L'Arche's Daybreak community in Toronto, Canada, one of the members of the community had died. Nouwen stepped quickly and naturally into the role of pastor. Later, steadily and quietly drawn towards the community, he decided to join permanently. Becoming a member of a community servicing the handicapped, Nouwen had to renounce the power, influence and gifted student body and faculty of Harvard.

At Daybreak, he lived among people who had never heard of his fame and had never read any of his books. It turned out to be the most important decision of his life. Some of his friends warned him that leaving Harvard was a mistake, but his longing for a new, more deeply spiritual life drove him to seek a place where, as Christ himself had desired, he could lay his head.

Perhaps Nouwen's woundedness created a need to bond with people. He could certainly do this at Daybreak, where the handicapped needed to be nurtured and loved as they are.

Home, of course, is an actual place; but it also is an inner sanctuary. Nouwen preferred this translation of John 15:4: "Make your home in me, as I make mine in you." We all need a home, a place to call our own, a place where we can be ourselves, where we have no need to wear masks. Such places can be destroyed by war, tornadoes, fire, and hurricanes, but there is an unshakable home within us: that sacred place where Christ abides. He is present within at every moment of our lives. In a second of attention, we need only turn our mind gently, to find him. He is there for us. Whenever we wish, we can commune with him. As Nouwen would say, he is our First Love and our Eternal Home.

Reflection Questions

Have I made my physical home a place of hospitality and peace? Have I opened my door to loved ones? Have I opened my inner home (heart) to my brothers and sisters, offering them a place of understanding, tolerance and love? Am I hospitable to strangers as well as to people I know and love? Are the doors of my inner home open to God?

7
Icons

Focus Point

////////////

Our culture often uses visual aids to win students'
attention. Nouwen understood their power in
prayer life as well. His own positive experience
taught him that icons lead to a deeper spiritual
life. However, they demand attention. Anyone
willing to devote attention to an icon, Nouwen
promises, will receive priceless gifts of grace.

////////////

*They (icons) do not reveal themselves to us at first
sight. It is only gradually after a patient, prayerful
presence that they start speaking to us. And as they
speak, they speak more to our inner than to our outer
senses. They speak to the heart that searches for
God.*

(*Behold the Beauty of the Lord,
Praying with Icons*, p. 14)

//////////

Nouwen's fine aesthetic sense drew him to art and its power to lift the human spirit — particularly to religious icons. During his visit to the L'Arche community at Trossly in 1983, Jean Vanier's assistant Barbara Swankekamp had placed Rublev's icon *The Holy Trinity* on a table in his room. He gazed at it throughout the many weeks of his stay, and when he visited again Swankekamp replaced that icon with another, *The Virgin of Vladimir*. Again, the mysterious beauty of the icon compelled him to gaze at it for long periods of time. Two other icons also moved him: Rublev's *The Savior of Zvenigorod* and *The Descent of the Holy Spirit*. He gradually came to understand that icons are windows on the divine, and he found that offering them undivided attention can be a tremendous aid in the spiritual life. Nouwen writes eloquently about all four icons in *Behold the Beauty of the Lord, Praying with Icons*.

In the West, the dominant spiritual message is to listen, but in the Orthodox world, it is to gaze attentively, thus the emphasis on icons in their religious tradition. Henri believed that patient devotion to an icon will generate a deep spiritual relationship. The icon serves as a bridge to the one gazed upon. For instance, an icon of Christ leads viewers to become Christ-centered. Looking attentively face-to-face with Christ leads to a deeper understanding of the Incarnation. Beyond mere abstract understanding of dogma, viewers become intimate with Christ, who is with them, and they with him. They become one with him. Unlike the apostles who fell asleep while Jesus endured the agony of Gethsemane, attentive gazing keeps us awake with Christ. Intense gazing offers the possibility of union: "It is no longer I who live, but it is Christ who lives in me" (Gal 2:20). Our attention to him during his agony in the garden expresses our love for him. As Plato has said, we become what we behold. By gazing upon Christ, we become more Christ-like in word and in deed.

The spiritual power of icons so intrigued (and entranced) Nouwen that he commissioned a well-known iconographer, Robert Lentz, to create a *Christus* for him. The beauty of an icon of Christ with St. John the Evangelist, painted not with the traditional pose of John's reclining his head on Jesus' chest but with John approaching the enthroned Christ in a humble, lovingly affectionate bow, had always impressed Lentz. With Nouwen's heartfelt approval, the artist created for him an icon with that image, which Nouwen came to call "Christ the Bridegroom." He placed it opposite his bed so that it was the first object he saw when he awakened and the last when he retired. This sacred icon became an important part of his life; he turned to it in times of anguish and distress, and in times of joy.

Nouwen commissioned an iconographer, but reputable religious shops offer affordable fine reproductions of famous icons, Western and Eastern alike. For that matter, anyone can create his or her own icon by taking up a brush and painting the Christ that arises from the heart. It may not turn out to be a masterpiece, but it will work its grace on the one who gazes upon it. It should be kept in a special place so that it can be turned to often, thereby coming closer to the Christ that abides within, closer to you than you are to yourself.

Icons provide spiritual grounding. Ancient icons, like those Nouwen admired, make viewers recall that they are eternal, that death is not their end. The very presence of a holy icon, in a corner of the home or in a bedroom, reaffirms faith. An icon proclaims that its image will outlive the artist in this world but not in the next. Icons also serve as reminders that prayer does not depend on words: gazing at a holy icon is prayer itself, probably more eloquent than any spoken prayer. As important as words are, a look of love is far superior to a declaration of love. The words "I love you" are easily pronounced without real meaning. In fact, "love" has been misused so often and so irresponsibly that to the modern ear it often creates suspicion. Eyes, however, are the windows of the soul; a look inspires safety and trust.

The Orthodox, for whom icons are an important part of their faith, pray while standing and with their eyes open, as did the early Christians. This stance allows them to remain open to their brothers and sisters without closing themselves within a personal, interior world. They kneel only during penitential prayer, and never during Eastertide. Keeping the eyes open so as to see brethren and to see icons is to be present to Christ — not only in the icons but within each neighbor. Each practicing Christian is an icon: "It is no longer I who live, but it is Christ who lives in me."

Thus, practicing gazing upon icons, honing skills in attention, leads to ever greater contact with the Christ within. By becoming more and more attentive to icons and their numinous message, those who pray transfer their attention more and more to the world and its people. Such prayer generates sensitivity to others' suffering, pain, anguish; like Christ, we can love them and do all we can to help them.

Seeing Georges Rouault's original paintings of Christ is a profound spiritual experience because the *sainte face* of Christ reveals the utter agony of His suffering as well as His supreme, eternal love for each person, captured in His humble submission and in His soulful eyes. His human face contains every person's pain, anguish, and even fears, for Jesus too was afraid, as revealed in the Garden of Gethsemane. But fear of his destiny and the agony he would have to endure did not stop him from embracing his Father's will.

Those who pray with icons cannot help but become more Christ-like. Surely this is what occurred with Henri Nouwen, a man of holy attention, a man who understood the power of icons to help him become a better Christian, a better human being. Had he not learned to pray with icons, he may not have been able to offer such sensitive attention to Adam, his real, human icon, whose twisted body he attended, bathed, dressed and fed, whose face he came to love more than any other.

Reflection Questions

Do I use icons in my prayer life? Have I purchased one of the affordable ones that are available? Have I tried to create my own icon, one that reflects my personal intimacy with God? Have I chosen a space or corner in my home where I can place an icon, a reminder to pray daily? Do I appreciate the word-icons of Christ found from the New Testament? Or word-icons like Herbert's "Love Bade Me Welcome"? Have I read the New Testament faithfully, the word-icon *par excellence*?

8
Friendship

Focus Point

////////////

There are three kinds of Love: Agape, Philia and Eros. Friendship is love. Some do not always feel comfortable that they, indeed, love their friends. Nouwen cherished his many, many friends, but when he expected from them what only God can give, he created serious problems not only for himself but also for them.

////////////

Allow your friends the freedom to respond as they are able to. Let their receiving be as free as your giving. Then you will become capable of feeling true gratitude.

(*The Inner Voice of Love*, p. 83)

////////////

Nouwen had a nervous breakdown precipitated by the end of a relationship with a friend who was deeply compassionate, sensitive, and sympathetic on almost every level. Nouwen had often experienced terrible loneliness, and had finally found someone with whom he experienced acceptance, affection and joy, someone whom he could depend upon for counsel and support.

He met Nathan Ball at the Daybreak community and they quickly befriended one another. Nouwen, a needy person, demanded much more than Nathan could satisfy. Suspending the friendship plunged Nouwen into a deep, debilitating depression. His co-workers and circle of other friends feared for his life and rushed him into therapy.

During his breakdown, a lifetime of anguish and rejection led his wounded child to emerge, crying for the touch, the caress, the nurturing that his well-meaning mother inadvertently had denied him. Nouwen would crawl into a fetal position on a bed, and his therapists would cradle him as they would a new born baby. They touched him back to life.

Ever the writer, Nouwen, even in his extreme psychological agony, summoned his artistic discipline to record his encounter with self-shadows in *The Inner Voice of Love: A Journey through Anguish to Freedom*. This painful book reveals Nouwen in all his naked vulnerability, a man nearly swallowed by the abyss.

Few writers have the courage to reveal their hurts, their fears, their insecurities, their longings, and their despair — their very souls. But by writing about his friendship and what it meant to him, Nouwen reached a part of himself that had too long abided in darkness. By doing so, he achieved spiritual insights that helped him to survive his dark night of the soul, thus becoming a model for anyone overtaken by darkness, teetering on the precipice, cornered by the unending demands of ego.

Nouwen candidly admitted that he felt God had abandoned him. Unable to depend on divine love, he fell into the abyss. Life had no meaning. He lost his appetite and wept uncontrollably. Not even his great love for people could lift his spirit. Even the beauty of art and music lost its power to move him. It gradually dawned on him, however, that the fault lay not outside but within: he finally admitted that he had demanded much too much. He sought from his best friend what only God can supply.

He thus stumbled upon a wise insight: every life contains a First Love and a Second Love. The First Love is God, the One who loves each person unconditionally. The Second Love is the one with whom an individual falls in love. The danger lies in expecting the Second Love to take the place that only the First Love can fill. Nouwen's own egregious mistake nearly destroyed him because he invested his whole self in a human relationship. He learned to allow friends the right *not* to be God, an insight that he often reiterated after recovering from his ordeal.

In short, he had idealized his friend, bestowing upon him God-like virtues when in fact he was a human being like any other. By doing so, Nouwen made himself dependent upon his friend, causing him to distance himself from Nouwen and from a role only God could play. The unfortunate mistake of interpreting his friend's withdrawal as rejection precipitated him into his breakdown. Fortunately, the relationship eventually mended and, both completely reconciled, Ball was present when Nouwen died.

They were able to reestablish their friendship because Nouwen embraced an important truth: God is the center of our lives. No person can be all powerful, all-loving, all-attentive. We have to battle our own demanding, often vociferous egos every day. It is easy to hurt people, including friends and family, inadvertently or deliberately. To avoid such behavior, Nouwen encourages attention to self, to motives and desires. Above all, he encourages prayer, through which it is possible to learn to lose the self and thus find the self, a paradox that must be lived out to be understood.

Reflection Questions

Do I appreciate my friends? Do I accept their love? Do I accept their constructive criticism? Do I express my love to them? Do I show them kindness? Do I help them through their difficult times? Do I explore ways to become a better friend? Am I faithful, or merely a fair-weather friend?

9
Henri Nouwen and Thomas Merton

Focus Point

////////////

Those who begin to take the spiritual life seriously must find themselves a spiritual director, but today's shortage of priests makes it harder and harder to find one. Books by masters like Henri Nouwen and Thomas Merton become the next best thing, something Nouwen recognized early on in his ministry. He had read Merton closely, and his attraction to Merton's spiritual way is apparent in Nouwen's own reading and writing. When he found his own spiritual legs, however, he followed his own path. That is what spiritual directors do: they enable those they guide to stand on their own two legs and point them in the right direction: always toward God.

////////////

I met him [Merton] only once. Yet thereafter, his person and work had such an impact on me, that his sudden death stirred me as if it were the death of one of my closest friends. It therefore seems natural for me to write for others about the man who has inspired me most in recent years.

(*Thomas Merton: Contemplative Critic*, p. 3)

////////////

*H*enri Nouwen, a spiritual master to thousands, if not millions, had a spiritual master himself: Thomas Merton. They once met briefly, but had Merton lived, Nouwen would likely have sought out the Trappist to be his spiritual director. Although a tragic accident cut Merton's life short, Nouwen still was able to seek counsel in Merton's many books.

One of the first books to address Merton's influence as a spiritual writer/director was Nouwen's *Thomas Merton: Contemplative Critic*. It contains a brief, incisive biography and samples of his best writing. Nouwen's admiration for Merton reveals itself in the journal he kept during his six months' sojourn at the Trappists' Genesee Abbey in New York.

Merton's move from narcissistic preoccupation with his own spiritual needs to an embrace not only of his own flawed humanity but also that of the human race impressed Nouwen. Ten

years after he had become a Trappist, Merton
finally felt proud of his own humanity. He
achieved this transformation, Nouwen noted,
through solidarity with the poor, the disenfranchised, and the marginal, a fruit of his courageous entrance into the depths of solitude and
silence where, as a cloistered monk — or as he so
candidly described himself, "a guilty bystander"
— he discovered his own woundedness, his own
marginal position in the world.

These two men led starkly different lives.
Nouwen's parents lived long into his adult life,
whereas Merton was left an orphan by the
age of sixteen when both his parents died of
cancer. Nouwen felt close to his mother, but
Merton's was distant, stinting and severe in
her display of affection. Nouwen had a strict
father; Merton's was doting. Nouwen was a
cradle Catholic, Merton a convert. During
World War II, Nouwen lived in Nazi-occupied
Holland, whereas Merton lived within the
safety of a Trappist abbey. Nouwen enjoyed
life as a pastor, but Merton sought out the
Trappists, a religious order with a rigidly indi-
vidualistic rule.

Nouwen was people-oriented, and considered
his vocation to be one of service to others. Merton,
imbued with *contemptus mundi* (contempt of
the world) entered the Abbey of Gethsemani
to devote his life to private contemplation. He

connected with the world by praying for it and encouraging others to do so as well.

Nouwen's desire to touch people's lives revealed itself in his abiding interest in psychology. Because he had come to realize that he, like so many of the people he addressed, was also wounded he shared his woundedness with his students and with his ever-growing audience. His ground-breaking *The Wounded Healer* encouraged priests and ministers to abandon their traditional distance in order to mingle among the people, to open their hearts to their fellow brothers and sisters.

From a distance, through books, Merton argued that every person is born contemplative, but to practice contemplation must incorporate more silence and solitude into life.

When books and speaking engagements overwhelmed him, Nouwen asked to stay at the Genesee Abbey and to live like the monks, rising at 2:00 A.M. for the first of the *Horae Canonicae*, Vigils, followed throughout the day by Lauds, Mass, None, Vespers and Compline.

Like Thomas Merton, he went to the Trappists to pray, to be alone with God, and to experience a deeper silence. Nouwen's diary of his experience at Genesee remains popular because in it he shares his frustrations, his anxieties, his anguish, his feelings of failure and of inferiority. This painfully honest book depicts a man who wanted to devote himself to monastic life but failed. He had hoped to discover his vocation there, but came to realize that he was not suited for such a life. He could not bring himself to set aside his almost genetic need to serve people.

The silence and solitude, however, helped him to understand his real vocation. He learned to make room in a busy life for silence and solitude; without it, he could not experience true prayer, which means listening to "the still, small voice." This was the greatest lesson that Nouwen learned from Merton — to sit still, to be alone and to listen attentively.

Reflection Questions

Have I sought out a spiritual director? Have I turned to my parish priests for counsel in my spiritual life? Have I read spiritual books, such as those of Nouwen and Merton? Have I considered keeping a diary as a way of finding greater self-knowledge?

10
Adam

////////////////

During his earthly ministry, Jesus touched countless hearts and minds. He also touched people's bodies, in many cases curing them of their physical and spiritual ailments. People need to be touched. Henri Nouwen touched his students' and readers' hearts, often transforming their lives. He also needed to touch people physically. Nouwen placed his hands on Adam not to demonstrate a point but to dress and feed a man who could do neither for himself. As a priest, Nouwen realized that to touch Adam was also to touch Christ, for to care for the least is to care for Jesus.

////////////////

Adam's humanity was not diminished by his disabilities. Adam's humanity was a full humanity, in which the fullness of love became visible for me, and for others who grew to know him.

(*Adam, God's Beloved*, p. 50)

////////////

*H*enri Nouwen relinquished his popularity as a teacher and Harvard's lofty academic atmosphere to live in a world of handicapped people at the L'Arche Daybreak Community, outside Toronto, Canada.

Why would he give up such a lucrative, influential and successful career? He needed a home. When Jean Vanier offered him one, Nouwen realized that he had been offered a once-in-a-lifetime opportunity to grow as a priest and as a person.

The handicapped people at Daybreak would not be dazzled by Nouwen's fame. They would see through any disguise or affectation; with their guileless eyes, they would see the true person before them. Nouwen did not need more fame, praise, or glowing attention; he needed to live in a low place, to go where people had not read his books, not heard his dazzling sermons, not seen him sign his books. They needed a priest to counsel them in their troubles, to soothe them in their fears and anxieties, to assist them in their woundedness. Nouwen willingly, humbly chose to serve them.

Nouwen was given the responsibility for one of Daybreak's most handicapped members, Adam.

By himself, Adam could not get dressed or eat or go to the bathroom; he had frequent, sudden seizures. Indeed, he depended on others to live.

At first, Nouwen could not figure how to do this job. He was restless, eager to begin his day, his work summoning him the moment he awakened. Adam slowed him down; Nouwen had to learn patience, to pay attention to another's physical and spiritual needs. Adam "taught" Nouwen not through the spoken or written word, but through the sacred text of his ravaged body and mind. He taught Nouwen about Christ through a spirituality of weakness.

Nouwen had to learn such lessons, which he had forgotten during his long sojourn among the privileged and powerful. He had become accustomed to engaging only the intellect. Adam taught Nouwen to enter the soul not through the mind but through the heart, to connect with others through touch and love.

Of course, Nouwen understood only too well that he was the least fit person to care for Adam. Always uncomfortable in his own body, he was self-conscious about his awkwardness; always on the go, he saw how his driven lifestyle might harm Adam. But he persevered. Despite these shortcomings as Adam's caregiver, Jean Vanier himself noted that Nouwen seized the opportunity to announce Adam to the world and to celebrate him.

At first, his responsibility in caring for Adam frightened Nouwen. Unsure about what was expected, he feared upsetting Adam. With the help of other assistants, caring for Adam became the most liberating experience of Nouwen's life. Such care, however, took time. Getting him up in the morning, into the bathroom, washed and clothed took two hours or more. Nouwen chafed at the slowness. He came to realize, however, what a privilege it was. A photograph of Nouwen with Adam recalls Michelangelo's *Pietà*. Like Mary cradling Christ in her arms, Nouwen cradles Adam in his.

Nouwen loved Adam and all the members of Daybreak, and they returned his love. *Adam, God's Beloved* reveals how Adam and Daybreak changed him. Even more than his life, however, Adam's death moved Nouwen profoundly. He reveals his poignant love in *Sabbatical Journey*, which was published after Nouwen's own death. Viewing Adam's lifeless body, Nouwen writes, "Here is my counselor, teacher, and guide, who never could say a word to me but taught me more than anyone else. Here is Adam, my friend, my beloved friend, the most vulnerable of all the people I have ever known and at the same time the most powerful."[1]

Reflection Questions

Have I appreciated the beauty of God's handicapped? Have I volunteered to help them or have I shied away? Have I realized that each handicapped person is special, each an icon of God?

11
The Cup of Life

Focus Point

////////////

The cup is one of the universal symbols for life in mythology, religion and poetry. It appears in the Psalms and in the gospel stories, particularly in accounts of the Last Supper. Jesus' using it as metaphor for life — a cup filled with all that human existence requires — moved Nouwen.

////////////

Drinking the cup of life involves holding, lifting, *and* drinking. *It is the full celebration of being human. Can we hold our life, lift our life, and drink it, as Jesus did? Just letting that question sink in made me feel very uncomfortable. But I knew that I had to start living with it.*

(*Can You Drink the Cup?*, p. 21)

////////////

*A*t his ordination, Nouwen received from his uncle Anton, himself a priest who had been ordained in 1922, a chalice made by a famous Dutch goldsmith. Its elaborate design, adorned with diamonds that had belonged to Nouwen's grandmother, included a crucifix shaped as a tree of life, with golden grapes and leaves gracing the node and bowl. Around the rim of the chalice was engraved: "*Ego sum vites, vos palmites*": "I am the vine, you are the branches."

His uncle presented it because Nouwen's ordination enhanced the family's honor. Nouwen often displayed the beautiful chalice to friends but he ceased using it when he realized it did not represent the life he wanted to live.

At Daybreak, he began to use a chalice designed by the glassblower Simon Pearce in Vermont. The way Nouwen's hands embraced the glass during Mass symbolized not only Christ's death and resurrection but also Nouwen's life, recalling St. Paul's words in Galatians: "It is no longer I who live, but it is Christ who lives in me" (2:20).

One of Nouwen's most moving books, *Can You Drink the Cup?*, takes its title from Matthew 20:20–23. When the mother of Zebedee's sons asked Jesus to promise that her sons would sit on the right and left sides of Jesus, he replied, "You do not know what you are asking. Are you able to drink the cup that I am about to drink?" The cup becomes a metaphor for the life we are asked to live. During a morning Eucharist at Daybreak with about twenty other people attending, Nouwen felt God speaking to him: " 'Can you drink the cup?' pierced my heart like the sharp spear of a hunter."[1] He realized that answering this question would change his life radically.

It comes as no surprise, then, that Nouwen would exchange his uncle's chalice for a simple, transparent glass cup. Gold adorned with diamonds does not represent Christ's humble poverty; at the last supper, he likely used a worn wooden cup, something pragmatic and utilitarian. Why glass? Like human beings, glass is fragile. It is also transparent, revealing its contents. Nouwen too was transparent: what you saw is what you got. He stepped down from the pedestal of priesthood to mingle among the people. He declined using an opulent chalice when so many of his flock at Daybreak were poor.

Although the elaborately adorned chalice fails to represent certain features of Jesus Christ, the goldsmith likely intended no contradiction; he probably felt that he was glorifying our Lord whose body and blood the cup would contain; should not divinity be contained in a cup of exquisite beauty?

Besides fragility and transparency, the glass cup also suggests omnipresence. Only the rich own gold and diamonds, but glass is common. Nouwen's choice of the glass cup represented the people with whom he identified: the weak, the poor, the fragile, the sick and the wounded.

The glass chalice also symbolizes his ministry. Glass must be held carefully, if not tenderly. One slip of the hand would dash it to pieces against the floor. A priest must treat people the same way. He must attend to the needs of his wounded, fragile people. He must handle them with extreme care, with *love*, as Jesus taught.

Nouwen recognized and understood people's pain, hurt, frustration, and anxiety. He understood that most (including himself) are wounded. He, therefore, treated each person with tender, loving attention. He would choose the right word, the saving word that each individual needed to hear. He held people in the tender gaze of his Christ-like love, cradling God's children gently, sensitively aware, from his own personal experience, that most things break.

Nouwen was drawn to the metaphor of the cup because it is an archetypal symbol of life. We must drink the cup we are offered, even though it sometimes is filled with sorrow and grief. Rejecting life's cup means denying our unique life as well as God's will.

Christ himself faced horrific fears. In the Garden of Gethsemane, he asked his Father,

"Remove this cup from me...." But he quickly continued, "... Yet, not what I want, but what you want" (Mk 14:36).

To drink the cup of life is to surrender to God's will. With the psalmist, we hope that our cup will overflow with good things. We must, however, accept the pain, the doubt, the fear, and ultimately the end of life. To do so is to follow the example of Jesus Christ.

Nouwen prayed for the grace to follow the will of God. He made every important decision only after a great deal of prayer. He knew that going to Daybreak, for instance, would be one of the most important and difficult decisions of his life, so he prayed fervently to be willing to drink the cup no matter what it contained.

The cup of Daybreak, he discovered, held both joy and suffering. He spent both his happiest days and the saddest there. His nervous breakdown while serving as pastor nearly destroyed him, but he drank his cup as Christ taught in the Garden of Gethsemane. Many were surprised that he survived his breakdown. He recovered, however, because through suffering he increased his self-knowledge. His life mirrored the poet Robinson Jeffers' insight, "Even in the bitter lees and sediment/New discovery may lie."[2] Paradoxically, his breakdown allowed a breakthrough to greater wisdom, helping him become a better priest, a better human being.

The priest who chose a fragile chalice understood that people are represented better by glass than by ostentatious, expensive gold.

Reflection Questions

Have I fallen into the trap of whining about my life? Am I angry at God for my life, not accepting responsibility for most of its unhappiness? Have I serenely accepted those things in my life that I cannot change? Have I changed those things that can be changed? Have I accepted the cup of life that God has offered? Have I drunk with gratefulness and joy? Am I willing to drink it to the lees?

12
The Still Center

Focus Point

////////////

Centered persons, as the saying goes, have their act together. Everyone wants to be centered, but many things can cause life be go out of balance. Nouwen's imbalance came from demanding too much from his friends. Because he did so, he jeopardized a cherished friendship and suffered a nervous breakdown. Even when life seems out of control, however, the still center is always there, awaiting God's presence.

////////////

Our inner sanctum, that inner, holy place, that sacred center in our lives, where only God may enter, that is as important for our lives as the domes are for the city of Rome.

(*Clowning in Rome*, p. 36)

////////////

*A*t home in the Netherlands, the large wagon wheels that decorated the entrances of farms or the walls of shops and restaurants fascinated Nouwen. The hub, strong spokes, and wide rim reminded him of the importance of living life from the center, the hub.

All cultures use the wheel as a symbol. In the West, it represents God, who has neither beginning nor ending. In the East, it represents life, the wheel upon which we all abide, constantly turning the past into the present, the present into the future.

The rim, Nouwen noted, touches only one spoke at a time. The hub, however, touches all of them at once. Life lived spoke-by-spoke is incomplete and unfocused. The full strength and power of the wheel lies at the hub. Strong people emulate the wheel living from the center, which is God.

The poems (*Four Quartets*) and plays (particularly *Murder in the Cathedral*) of T.S. Eliot use the image of the wheel. For him the center is eternity and the rim of the wheel is present, past and future time. We all live, he suggests, on the rim, in time which is always moving. Certain people, however, penetrate to the still center of the wheel: holy people, saints, who move there through selflessness and are graced with a glimpse of God.

Nouwen devoted his life to finding the still center. At first, he spent too much time with the spokes. He preached wherever he was invited. He took up numerous writing projects. Even though they were the best in America, he hop-scotched from one college to another. He was always on the go, living not from the center, but on the rim.

He learned about living from the center the hard way. First, while walking on an icy road in Canada, he was hit by a passing van's extended mirror. The impact broke five ribs and ruptured his spleen, which had to be removed. This near-death experience made him reevaluate his life. In the solitude of the hospital, he realized that his life was restless and uncentered, overwhelmed with speaking and writing books. He needed to slow down, to give more time to prayer, more time to God.

He had placed friendship, not God, at the hub of his life. He expected his friends to fill the place only God can fill. Some became weary and wary of his neediness; Nouwen interpreted their honest and valid responses as rejection. When he placed Nathan Ball at the center of his life, Nouwen came crashing down. His suffering taught him that only God can fill the space of the hub, the center. Placing another human being in that sacred space leads to delusion and invites chaos, not to mention the injustice of demanding that another person supply what only God can fulfill.

It is a familiar trap, putting at the center of life false gods: money, jobs, friendship, sex, power. Life knocks the fortunate down and while flat on their backs, they win a new perspective. They come to perceive their fragmentation, their delusional reliance on false values and realize that they truly want not fragments, not falseness, but wholeness.

Everyone aspires, consciously or unconsciously, to become whole. Carl Jung was intrigued by the symbol of wholeness, the *circle*. Quoting Saint Bonaventure, he defined God as "... a circle, whose center is everywhere and whose circumference is nowhere."[1] In the circle, he finds an archetype for the structure of the psyche, with the Self at the center of the psyche. In Western culture, he claimed, the Self is Christ.

His mistakes, and he admits to many, taught Nouwen to live from the center. He came to understand that Christians find happiness by living in imitation of Christ: the meaning and the substance of life lies in the example of Jesus Christ. Keeping Jesus in the mind and soul enables life not from the rim but from the center. Life at the rim is superficial but a centered life is authentic and whole, in touch with God.

Reflection Questions

Have I strived to discover the still center within me? Or am I too involved with getting and spending? Am I running away from God? Am I centered? If not, why not? Is Christ at the center of my life? Can I say, "It is no longer I who live, but it is Christ who lives in me" Can I pray, "Not my will but yours be done."

13
Writing

Focus Point

////////////

Everyone needs an outlet, such as gardening, knitting, cooking, reading. Nouwen found his in writing. He wrote all the time, and little in his life did not become grist for one of his books. In writing he was able to lose himself, but he was also able to find himself. By writing he reached self-knowledge.

////////////

I become more and more aware that for me writing is a very powerful way of concentrating and of clarifying for myself many thoughts and feelings. Once I put my pen on paper and write for an hour or two, a real sense of peace and harmony comes to me.

(*Genesee Diary,
Report from a Trappist Abbey*, p. 121)

////////////

*H*enri Nouwen was not a born writer like Thomas Merton. At his core, he was a priest. Next he was a teacher. As a professor of pastoral theology at Yale Divinity School, he prepared his lectures in three parts, like a three-act play. He would often ask his students to read and critique them. His first books were produced through such collaboration.

In time, Nouwen realized he had a calling not only to preach and to lecture but also to write. His style reflects his eloquent and powerful personality. Most of his books are still in print, with a large and faithful following that increases day by day.

His writing is simple, lucid and transparent, marked by familiar diction. Although steeped in psychology and mystical theology, Nouwen deliberately avoided academic jargon. He sought to communicate with readers from every background. His simple sentences, however, convey insight and wisdom that are far from simple.

Nouwen possessed the gift of lucidity, of rendering difficult concepts so clear that anyone could understand them. "Lucid" derives from the Latin *lux*, light. Every book Nouwen ever wrote tried to shed light on the spiritual life in order to bring readers closer to Christ, the Light of the world.

Readers flock to Nouwen's books because in them they find themselves. He fearlessly shared his inner doubt, anguish, fear and loneliness. Because he wrote from his heart, his words resonate with others' hearts, mirroring not only his experience but theirs.

Nouwen did not conceal himself behind masks of pretence, affectation, or ego, but revealed his vulnerability, humility and truth. He is a human being like any other, and for that readers love him and his heartfelt message. He surely does not live in an ivory tower distant from human cares and problems. Quite the opposite: he mingles, his hand always extended to help and to guide.

Nouwen also wrote to discover himself. It helped him to clarify his thoughts, to discover the roots of his inner struggles, to find answers to his questions, his doubts — in short, to understand the meaning of his life. For instance, writing *Genesee Diary* led Nouwen to realize that his vocation was not monastic. His struggles with solitude, silence and prayer sapped his energy, turmoil and confusion captured in his diary. Writing about his difficulties at the monastery, interior as well as communal, made him understand that he was not cut out to live as a monk. He discovered that he could not be Thomas Merton; he could only be himself. God had different plans for him.

Later in his life, his nervous breakdown led Nouwen to enter therapy. His therapists helped him tremendously. His best therapy, however, was his writing. His journal of a dark night of the soul, filled with rejection, love, loneliness and woundedness, healed him.

Writing is demanding, a form of asceticism. Nouwen found his best time for writing in the morning, when he was quiet and alone. All writers know the terror of the blank page. Nouwen, however, rarely suffered from writer's block. He was old-fashioned, writing in longhand, using a fountain pen. Nouwen wrote an amazing number of books, but even more amazingly he wrote not in his native language but in English, a testament to his gifts as a communicator.

The blank page was his friend, a friendship that led him to discover God's purpose for him: to spread the message of the gospel through the written word. Like his hands, his books touched the suffering, the grieving, the lonely, the fearful, the abandoned. Through his books his hands still reach across time to readers in their Now moments, to help and to guide, particularly in dark times.

Nouwen's books have been translated into many languages. A friend of his who had visited Bosnia just after the war there related a fascinating story about one of them. A group visiting the rubble of a church destroyed in a battle spied a book amidst the debris. The title was obscured, but someone figured out that it was a Croatian edition of *Letters to Marc about*

Jesus. Nouwen had not even known that it had been translated. Hearing this story gave him joy because it had not interested the nephew for whom he had written it. This event made him understand that his book indeed had found its readers, that it had achieved the purpose God had in mind.

Nouwen's books still find readers worldwide. Hillary Clinton named *The Return of the Prodigal Son* as one of her favorite books. Her compliment demonstrates the universality of Nouwen's appeal to people beyond boundaries of every gender, faith, or nationality.

Reflection Questions

Do I have an emotional outlet? Have I cultivated a hobby? Do I have a way to lose myself in order to recharge myself with energy? Have I strived to discover my latent abilities? Have I taken advantage of spiritual books, including the Bible?

14
Death

Focus Point

////////////

Nouwen first faced personal grief at his mother's death. He was unprepared, and his mourning was long and painful. For the first time, he realized his own vulnerability. The experience provoked serious reflection on facing and accepting death, not only that of friends and relatives but also the inevitability of his own, including life's innumerable small "deaths": losing friendships, jobs, homes, possessions, and health.

////////////

It seems indeed important that we face death before we are in any real danger of dying and reflect on our mortality before all conscious and unconscious energy is directed to the struggle to survive.

(*A Letter of Consolation*, p. 28)

////////////

*T*hose who pay attention to the many guises in which it comes can learn the wisdom of not fearing death. Nouwen first experienced death when his mother succumbed to cancer. It dealt him a devastating blow for which he was unprepared. He grieved terribly. He shed so many tears, mourned so piteously that one of his brothers was moved to say that he had never seen a son so stricken by the loss of a mother.

Nouwen had faced death before, but the encounters were less personal and intense. Leaving his family, friends and country to study in America was a kind of death. He had to assimilate a new culture and way of life, a task particularly challenging during the counter-cultural movement of the 1960s and 1970s that had turned life in America upside down. Nouwen courageously embraced the turmoil, struggles, confusion and excitement of a culture transforming itself.

Nouwen embraced America because he did not fear the unknown. With eyes wide open, he left a successful position at Notre Dame for Yale Divinity School. Although he was able to publish a book a year at Yale, he gladly accepted the challenge of a professorship at Harvard Divinity School even though it meant leaving once again the known, especially friends and colleagues. When Jean Vanier offered him a home at L'Arche, he again left the known for a world he had never experienced before, to which he would have to learn new ways of adapting.

Each move into the unknown allowed Nouwen to grow as a teacher, preacher, priest and person. He understood that the crux of a full life is change, and even when terrified he embraced it fully and appreciatively.

In Canada, he had a near-death experience. He had already experienced the death of a cherished friendship (which was eventually mended). Life had put other lessons about death in Nouwen's path, and as an astute student he learned his lessons well. He learned most, however, from the trapeze act of the Rodleigh family, who Nouwen admired. Their finely tuned airy acrobatics led him to a new, life-transforming theology that he hoped one day to write about. He died before he could produce that book, but interspersed throughout his other writings are gems of insight won from observing as well as conversing with the Rodleighs.

The leader of the trapeze group told Nouwen, "As a flyer, I must have complete trust in my catcher. The public might think that I am the great star of the trapeze, but the real star is Joe, my catcher. He has to be there for me with split-second precision and grab me out of the air as I come to him in the long jump."

Nouwen prompted him, "How does it work?"

"The secret," Rodleigh said, "is that the flyer does nothing and the catcher does everything. When I fly to Joe, I have simply to stretch out my arms and hands and wait for him to catch me and pull me safely over the apron behind the catchbar."

"You do nothing?"

"Nothing."[1]

This brief exchange led Nouwen to a theology of life and of death. Surrender yourself to God, our catcher. He will catch us during life's airy leaps and flights; He will also catch us in our greatest leap, into the darkness of death. Like the speaker in Francis Thompson's poem *The Hound of Heaven*, Nouwen believed he would hear God's voice say, "Rise, clasp My hand, and come!"[2]

Reflection Questions

Do I allow myself to think about death? Have I been running away from death? Have I been sensitive to friends who have lost loved ones to death? Have I been living so that when death comes, I will be prepared to accept it? Or do I put it off living? At the time of death, will I find that I have not lived fully?

15
Prayer

Focus Point

////////////

Prayer can take place anywhere, anytime. Henri Nouwen learned this truth from a lifetime of praying as a son, a seminarian, a priest, a teacher and a care-giver. Life itself becomes a prayer if every thought and action is dedicated to God. We can do this the moment we awaken, offering ourselves and our day to God.

////////////

To be continually in communion with God does not mean thinking about God in contrast to thinking about other things, nor does it mean spending time with God instead of spending time with other people.

(*Clowning in Rome*, p. 67)

////////////

*L*ike his spiritual mentor, Thomas Merton, Henri Nouwen was a man of deep prayer. The foremost prayer for him was the celebration of the Eucharist. He said the Mass with exquisite attention, every word and action as beautiful and holy as an icon. Like Christ in George Herbert's "Love Bade Me Welcome," Nouwen is a loving, welcoming host of the Eucharist. Herbert writes,

Love (3)

Love bade me welcome: yet my soul drew back,
　　Guilty of dust and sin.
But quickeyed Love, observing me grow slack
　　From my first entrance in,
Drew nearer to me, sweetly questioning
　　If I lacked anything.

A guest, I answered, worthy to be here:
　　Love said, thou shalt be he.
I, the unkind, ungrateful? Ah my dear,
　　I cannot look on thee.
Love took me by the hand, and smiling did reply,
　　Who made the eyes but I?

True, Lord, but I have marred them: let my
　　shame
　　Go where it deserves.
And dost thou not know, says Love, who bore
　　the blame?

My dear, then I will serve.
Thou must sit down, says love, and taste my
    meat:
    So I did sit and eat.

At Daybreak, Nouwen celebrated Mass for
the staff and the handicapped residents. Some
often burst out in ungodly noises. At first, this
disturbed Nouwen, who relished the deep,
contemplative prayer during the quiet portions
of the Mass. But he gradually learned to tol-
erate and then to accept the sounds from his
new flock, gladly accepting their "joyful noise
unto the Lord." Prayer certainly includes the
elegant delivery of a highly educated priest,
but it can also be as humble and simple as saying Abba: Father. Even an ordinary grunt can
be like incense rising to a loving God.

The way he celebrated Mass revealed the
depth of Nouwen's prayer. He uttered each
word with reverence, performed each gesture
with grace. Raising the cup became an act of
supreme worship, Nouwen lovingly holding it
in his large, expressive hands, lifting the Body
and Blood of our Lord.

Except when grasping the cup, he held his
hands open, never closed. He wrote, "When
you are invited to pray, you are asked to open
your tightly clenched fist and give up your last
coin."[1] The coin represents the self: the one

who prays must surrender self, become ego-less.

The Mass is the ultimate Christian prayer, but there are also other ways of praying. Gazing upon the beauty of art can be prayer.[2] Nouwen admired artistic expression, especially the works of van Gogh and Rembrandt. He examined van Gogh's letters to his brother Theo. Unlike the brothers in the parable of the prodigal son, Vincent and Theo loved each other uncondi-tionally. Without Theo's help Vincent would have perished long before he did. Theo loved, respected and esteemed his brother's genius, never hesitating to supply financial and emo-tional support.

Nouwen studied Vincent's letters as if they were sacred texts. In many ways they indeed were, as they revealed Vincent's love of Jesus and his love for the poor. Nouwen was moved by Vincent's early attempts to become a minis-ter, but in the end, the artist had to accept the fact that he was not called to become a Christian minister.

Vincent's love for the poor, the exploited, the disenfranchised led Nouwen to support social causes of the poor, particularly victims of racism in America. He participated in the Civil Rights March to Washington. At Martin Luther King's funeral, Nouwen joined the

funeral cortege. He gave credit to the influence
of Vincent van Gogh, a spiritually eloquent
artist, for his empathy with the oppressed.

As mentioned in the meditation for Day One
of this volume, Rembrandt's *The Return of the
Prodigal Son* also inspired Nouwen. Its beauty
and message became the focus of lengthy
intellectual and emotional contemplation.
Rembrandt's depiction of the Father's love for
his lost son led Nouwen for the first time to
understand the importance of fatherhood.

At first, he identified with the spendthrift son,
who ended up feeding pigs. But he also identified with the son who resented his father's lavish
display of love. Nouwen, himself an eldest son,
often felt, like the elder son in the parable, that
he had somehow failed his father. Then one day
a friend reminded Nouwen that as a priest he
was called to be a father.

Catholics call priests "Father." As a priest,
Nouwen was called to father the L'Arche community and all who came for spiritual counsel.
The strained relationship with his own father
made it difficult for him to see himself in that
capacity, but with effort he finally was able
to assume the responsibilities inherent in his
vocation.

The Mass and the contemplation of beauty,
whether visual or verbal, become prayer if we

surrender ourselves to the point of self-forgetting. Simone Weil defined such an act in this fashion: "Absolutely unmixed attention is prayer."[2] The Bible also teaches how to pray. While pondering the Annunciation, Nouwen discovered what he claimed is the best paradigm of prayer — Mary silently listening to the words of the angel Gabriel. At first, they frighten her. After listening, she ponders, both acts of prayer. But the third step is the most important — she surrenders herself to God: "Here am I, the servant of the Lord; let it be with me according to your word" (Lk 1:38). The stages of prayer are simple: listening, pondering, and surrendering. It is not difficult. The desire to do so allows prayer anywhere and anytime. From the beginning of his life Nouwen was blessed; even as a boy he played at being a priest because he wanted to pray.

Emulating his life will allow us to achieve the primary purpose of prayer, closeness to God. We achieve the secondary purpose when we perform intercession, praying for our brothers and sisters in Christ in this life and in the next.

Reflection Questions

Do I pray? Do I pray enough? Do I like to read books about prayer, but fail to put their counsel into practice? Do I set aside time in my life for private prayer? Do I begin and end my day with prayer? Do I understand that prayer is not only repeating sacred words? Do I understand that gazing upon beauty or simply waiting in silence to hear the "still, small voice" of God is prayer?

Notes

Day 4: Van Gogh

1. Cliff Edwards, *van Gogh and God, A Creative Spiritual Quest,* Foreword (Chicago: Loyola University Press, 1989), p. 32

2. Ibid., p. x.

Day 10: Adam

1. Henri Nouwen, *Adam, God's Beloved* (Maryknoll, NY: Orbis Books, 1997), p. 105

Day 11: The Cup of Life

1. Henri Nouwen, *Can You Drink the Cup?* (Notre Dame: Ave Maria Press, 1996), p. 20.

2. Robinson Jeffers, *Rock and Hawk, A Selection of Shorter Poems by Robinson Jeffers,* compiled and edited by Robert Hass (New York: Random House, 1987), p. 272.

Day 12: The Still Center

1. *Bonaventure: The Soul's Journey into God, The Tree of Life, The Life of St. Francis,* translation and introduction by Ewert Cousins (New York: Paulist Press, 1978), p. 100.

Day 14: Death

1. *Our Greatest Gift* (San Francisco: HarperCollins, 1994), p. 67.

2. Francis Thompson, *Poems of Francis Thompson* (New York: The Century Co., 1932), p. 81.

Day 15: Prayer

1. Henri Nouwen, *With Open Hands* (Notre Dame: Ave Maria Press, 1972), p. 21.

2. Simone Weil, *Simone Weil, An Anthology*, edited and introduced by Sean Miles (New York: Grove Press, 1986), p. 212.

Bibliography

Adam (Maryknoll, NY: Orbis, 1997).

A Letter of Consolation (New York: HarperOne, 1982).

Bread for the Journey, A Daybook of Wisdom and Faith (New York: HarperOne, 1997).

Can You Drink the Cup? (Notre Dame: Ave Maria, 1996).

Clowning in Rome (New York: Doubleday, 1979).

Here and Now, Living in the Spirit (New York: Crossroad, 1994).

Intimacy (New York: HarperCollins, 1969).

Lifesigns (New York: Doubleday, 1986).

Life of the Beloved (New York: Crossroad, 1992).

Making All Things New (New York: Harper & Row, 1981).

Reaching Out (New York: Doubleday, 1975).

Sabbatical Journey (New York: Crossroad, 1998).

Spiritual Journals (New York: Continuum, 1998).

The Inner Voice of Love (New York: Doubleday, 1998).

The Return of the Prodigal Son (New York: Doubleday, 1992).

The Selfless Way of Christ (Maryknoll, NY: Orbis, 2007).

The Way of the Heart (San Francisco: HarperCollins, 1981).

The Wounded Healer (New York: Doubleday, 1979).

Van Gogh and God, Cliff Edwards with Foreword by Henri Nouwen (Chicago: Loyola University Press, 1989).

With Burning Hearts (Maryknoll, NY: Orbis Books, 1994).

With Open Hands (Notre Dame: Ave Maria Press, 1972).

Saint Francis de Sales *(Claude Morel)*
978-0764-805752, paper

Saint Jeanne Jugan *(Michel Lafon)*
978-1-56548-329-3, paper

Saint John of the Cross *(Constant Tonnelier)*
978-0764-806544, paper

Saint Eugene de Mazenod *(Bernard Dullier)*
978-1-56548-320-0, paper

Saint Louis de Montfort *(Veronica Pinardon)*
978-0764-807152, paper

Saint Martín de Porres: A Saint of the Americas *(Brian J. Pierce)*
978-0764-812163, paper

Meister Eckhart *(André Gozier)*
978-0764-806520, paper

Thomas Merton *(André Gozier)*
978-0764-804915, paper

Saint Elizabeth Ann Seton *(Betty Ann McNeil)*
978-0764-808418, paper

Johannes Tauler *(André Pinet)*
978-0764-806537, paper

Saint Teresa of Ávila *(Jean Abiven)*
978-0764-805738, paper

Saint Thomas Aquinas *(André Pinet)*
978-0764-806568, paper